I Feel Surreal

Writing from the Ridge Kids
workshop at the Brooklyn
Public Library,
Bay Ridge Branch

2011

NYWC
New York Writers Coalition

Editors: Barbara Cassidy, Nancy L. Weber
Layout: Nancy L. Weber
Illustrations: Ridge Kids
Cover illustration: Tristan Leone

I Feel Surreal contains writing by the 2010-2011 members of the NY Writers Coalition Ridge Kids creative writing workshops conducted at the Brooklyn Public Library, Bay Ridge Branch. The library is an after-school sanctuary for the young people of this dynamic ethnically and culturally diverse community.

NY Writers Coalition thanks the following supporters, without whom this writing workshop and anthology would not exist: Amazon.com, Brooklyn Community Foundation, Kalliopeia Foundation, Mary Duke Biddle Foundation, the NYC Department of Cultural Affairs, Two West Foundation, the Union Square Awards, the WellMet Group, and all our individual donors and attendees of our annual Write-A-Thon.

NY Writers Coalition Inc. is a not-for-profit organization that provides free creative writing workshops for unheard New Yorkers. For more information about NY Writers Coalition Inc.:

NY Writers Coalition Inc.
80 Hanson Place, #603
Brooklyn, NY 11217
(718) 398-2883

info@nywriterscoalition.org
www.nywriterscoalition.org

For more information on the Brooklyn Public Library,visit
www.brooklynlibrary.org.

Introduction

I have been leading creative writing groups through NY Writers Coalition at the Bay Ridge Library for almost seven years. It has been a wonderfully rewarding experience for me, and has taught me among other things, that yes, you can make some difference in your community and ultimately the world, by actually trying. It took me a bit of time to get to that.

It has been a pleasure working with the children of Bay Ridge, Sunset Park and Dyker Heights through NYWC and I am eternally grateful to Aaron Zimmerman, Deborah Clearman, Nancy Weber and Erin Hopkins for that opportunity.

I would also like to thank the folks at the Bay Ridge Library-Yvonne Zhou, the tireless Christopher Lassen, Carl Fossum, Chris Bruni, Teresa Migut, and especially my assistants in Ridge Kids- Sarah Dobrowolski, Inga Nikitina, and Jessica Siwiec for all their hard work. I have an amazing group of writers this year and many thanks to them for just being themselves . Also, thanks to their parents for bringing them to the writing workshop each week.

My Thursdays are delightful.

Barbara Cassidy
May 2011

I FEEL SURREAL
HANNA PUELLE, AGE 6

When my brother looked like a monster in the
    water,
When a cat starts to talk,
A fish starts to dance,
When a ceiling board jumped,
When a slide banged itself,
When I jumped without even trying to jump,
When hair jumped on my head,
When clothes came out of my dresser like magic,
When a shoe jumped out of the closet,
When the shirt danced,
A chair jumped,
And a box covered my face,
When a pen danced,
When a bracelet jumped out of an earring,
A table with books and pens on it moved side to
    side,
When a book jumped up and down,
A bird flew into a deserted house,
A phone ordered what we wanted itself,
A leaf jumped off its tree when the wind wasn't
    even blowing,
When I flew in the air and I grew wings,
When the light jumped off the ceiling.

PEOPLE WHO THOUGHT THE OCTOPUS HAD THINGS THAT IT REALLY DID NOT
CHE ANDRADE, AGE 5

I don't have a mouth.
And people think I do have a mouth.
And people think I have six legs but I really don't.
And people think I have a nose but I really don't.
And people think I go to school, but I really don't.
And people think I have a tail, but I really don't.

FUN DAYS, DULL DAYS
CHE ANDRADE, AGE 5

An exciting afternoon is

Hugging my daddy,
Kissing my mama,
When I go to school.

A dull afternoon is

When my mom has to talk on the phone,
Just sitting on my bed,
Doing my homework.

THE CANDLE
KATE BAMBERG, AGE 9

A candle
Flames burning brightly
Lighting up dark days
Scents wafting towards me
I could watch
The flame for hours
But I am tired
So I blow it out
And fall asleep.

STRANGE FEELINGS
EVANGELINA BAUSO, AGE 8

I hear a monster swearing.
I smell fire.
I feel a person dying.
It is cool. I see rain and cars.
I taste crackers.

Now the weird part.
I hear screaming.
I feel blood.
I smell crazy people.
I see snow.
It is cool.
I taste, listen.

I hear a bell.
I smell metal.
I taste sour.
It is weird.
I see a church.

I hear music.
It is cool.
I see blank faces.

I hear a baby screaming.
He is crazy.
I hear a crazy person.
He is weird.
It is creepy.
It feels squishy! SSSSSSS

This is how I call sounds,
        but there is one more...listen.

I hear a person whistling he is an
        angel but weird.

So figure out what I heard.
Lucy's answer: I hear a baby screaming.

SURPRISES
GALILEE BEST, AGE 7

A surprise is

A gift,

Apples,

A pet,

A trip,

A picnic,

A show.

AQUA
GALILEE BEST, AGE 8

Aqua warms me up when I feel down in the
    dumps.
It fills up my heart with joy and happiness.
It is like a best friend you can really trust.
It's the color of the water at the beach.
It's smooth like sand and silky like sand through
    your hands.
It's like a spa just relaxing and tanning in the sun.
It's like doing martial arts and hearing the breeze
    of the wind.

MY IMPORTANT THINGS
GALILEE BEST, AGE 8

Pencils, erasers, paper, and computers are
    important for writers.
Chalkboards are important for teachers.
Clocks are important to tell time.
Toilets are important so people do not urinate their
    clothes.
Telephones are important so people can
    communicate to each other in far disasters.
Libraries are important because people can check
    out books.
And sisters are important to count on.

WHAT I HEAR
GALILEE BEST, AGE 8

I hear a babbling brook sing its name. I see the
babbling brook swaying side to side. I feel it
slipping through my hands. I smell the soothing
brook. I hear a train passing by. I see it pushing
smoke out its top. I feel the tin of the train. I hear
a clock saying tick-tock. I see Great Ben ticking.
I hear people dancing. I see guitars. I hear babies
crying. I see me as a child. I feel a pacifier in my
mouth. I hear a kid screaming. I see me having a
tantrum. I feel being in a punishment. I hear kids
laughing and screaming. I see them running and
walking. I feel a nice comfortable place. I hear
nature soothing and clear. I see a beautiful bird
chirping a song that calms me peacefully. I feel all
my senses. I can only write, but that doesn't mean
I am not bright.

MY TRIP TO LINCOLN CENTER
MEAGHAN BONDI, AGE 9

First thing you need to know about my field trip
with the class was the class only went here
because two of the thirty-two kids in my class are
in *The Nutcracker.*
The second thing you need to know is that Fiona is
Maria or Clara, and Megan is an angel and a main
party girl.
The third thing you need to know is that Liam,
Trevor, Russell, Justin, and Timewarp made fun of
Fiona because in the play she was married to a
prince or whatever.

The fourth and last thing you need to know is most
of the class liked the show,

and

I loved the show.

DEAR DIALGA
MEAGHAN BONDI, AGE 9

Dear Dialga,

I heard you can transport people out of time. Can you do it to me? I want to go to 72nd St PS 102 school, 90 years back. And then 20,000 years ahead. I think that would be really nice of you, for a Pokemon. My dad calls you a Pokeman.

Love,
Meaghan Bondi   :) :(

MARYGOLD
VERONICA BONDI, AGE 7

I am a gardener who is soothed by the sounds of birds chirping and the aroma of the flowers. Growing up in a rain forest I know all about plants everywhere. I'm all about plants and read all day and night about plants. When I am not reading I'm caring for my garden. I might even be at work. The cactus plant's needles don't prickle my skin. I think the plants that smell bad, smell good. I have 4,000,000,097,374 friends.

O HOMEWORK
VERONICA BONDI, AGE 7

O homework!

You're mean and selfish, definitely unkind.

Cause when I do you,

You mean, mean homework,

I want to hit you,

Tear you to pieces,

Put you to death,

Let the sink splash

Water on you.

I wish you would disappear.

Schoolwork, schoolwork,

I had enough.

Why do homework,

If we have schoolwork?

ALL I AM
VERONICA BONDI, AGE 7

I am sweet. I am playful.
I am made of reading.
I am made of friendship.
I am athletic,
I am the jewels of amethyst.
I am really fast.
I am made of pistachio ice cream (no nuts!)
I am made of bright blue morning glories.
I am made of the shining sunshine.
I am made of flowers blooming.
I am very healthy.
I am full of color.
I am made of sweets.
I am full of punctuation.
I am pink and purple.
I like pink, purple and aquamarine!
I am made of scary tales, biting, fighting
        werewolves beware!
I am peppermints burning bright!
I am made of dresses.
I am made of boots.
I am made of jewelry.
I am made of fun.
I am made of a lot of stuff,
Fun, exciting, more or less.
You see this is it!
That's all, bye!

UNTITLED
JASMIN BRACERO, AGE 6

I know the library.

I come here to read books and do writing class in
the library.

In the library is fun and in writing class I get to
write.

I know more learning in the library.

There are computers.

They also have movies.

They also have tables.

They have lots of books.

I love the library.

UNTITLED II
JASMIN BRACERO, AGE 6

The boy was playing with the ball and then he
        swam in the river.
And the snake was sleeping and he woke up and
        snuck.
Maybe a fight with the boy.

LAVENDER IS
MAEVE BRENNAN, AGE 6

Lavender is nice.
Lavender is cool.
Lavender is the sunset.
Lavender feels like silky hair.
Lavender smells like chocolate.
Lavender tastes like Oreos.
Lavender sounds like Irish stepdancers.
Lavender reminds me of the rainbow that
        I saw in Arizona two days in a row.
Lavender is the best.

THE FOUR SENSES
LUCY BYCHKOV, AGE 7

I hear guns all over
I see people in the army
I smell donuts from my mom
I taste blackberries
I like the sound

I hear people talking
I see a baseball game
I smell garbage
I taste pizza
I like that sound

I hear a bell
I see a person ringing it
I smell gold
I taste salt
I love the sound

I hear music
I see a band
I smell apples
I taste you
I really like it

I hear crying
I see a baby
I smell my fun
I taste fur
I like everything

I HAVE A DREAM
ROCHELLE CHIN, AGE 9

Written 4pm probably
I have a dream that my best friend Amanda moved
 back to New York.*
I have a dream that everything was free for me and
 nice people.
I have a dream that I had a mansion and a flying
 car.
I have a dream that I lived everywhere in the U.S;
There were 50 clones of me and sometimes I'd call
 them over to do 1,000,000 pages of
 home work- 20,000 pages each.
I have a dream that I'm eating chocolate.
I have a dream that I'm drinking water.
I have a dream I liked long division (which I do.)
I have a dream nobody was a maniac murderer.
I have a dream that Lazy Liam was in jail.
I have a dream there were couches in the elevator
 and a slide to go down.
I have a dream I was a famous author.
I have a dream I wouldn't have to look at my
 brother's butt.
I have a dream that my sister, Christy was 5.
I have a dream –oops I forgot! Oh yeah, I like
 baseball. (It's true.)
I have a dream there were purple birdies.

*From last year, sadly moved to Maryland. She
laughed at everything I said.

p.s. Lazy Liam always reads and he'll read for
eternity, no matter what he does, even going to the
bathroom or driving which he does with his feet,
and he's to run over tiny teddy bears.
p.p.s. Poor little teddy bear so innocent, cuddly
creatures.
He has to sit next to me.

A POEM IS
ROCHELLE CHIN, AGE 9

A poem is a monkey jumping on Amanda's head.

A poem is Kathy making an angry face.
(It looks funny.)

A poem is girly earrings. (I will never get my ears
pierced.)

A poem is Kathy going to violin.

A poem is I'll finish this later.

OTA
CHRISTINA ECONOMAKOS, AGE 7

Ota is a type of color
Orange, Green, Blue
It is very popular
It is really nice
It smells like cherries and apples
And a surprise of Blue Birds
Or a candy surprise
A very nice dog
A very nice bird in the sun
A little little green and some love and care
And a blue Ota is like a clue I love
And blue, black, green
And anything bubbling in my heart
It is better then
It goes around in a circle
And is a great big thing
I have never seen before
And a great big song I like
It is a great thing to see and smell and hear
So be nice, try to be nice
Ota is great
I think, I think.

COSTUME
CHRISTINA ECONOMAKOS, AGE 7

Rapunzel, Rapunzel let down your hair.
Batman slide to her rescue, Superman fly,
Wonderwoman save the day.
Ariel swims, Belle go and get the beast.
Werewolf goes to Transylvania, Vampires go and
    suck blood.
Mummy take off your toilet paper, somebody has
    to go to the bathroom.
Mummy can I have some toilet paper?
Bees go to the flowers.
Butterflies go to the flowers too.
Shrek go into the mud.
Cat girl go and rob a bank.
Fiona gets locked in a tower.
Joker fights the Batman.
Baseball players go trick-or-treating.
Vampire have I mentioned my name is Garlic?
Ghosts go through the wall.
I love Halloween.

JOHN WASHINGTON THE LIAR
STAVROULA ECONOMAKOS, AGE 9

John Washington in 1776 invented time traveling.
He wanted to go back to caveman time.

Everyone said he could not do it, but he knew he could do it. He tried to build a time traveler and each time he failed. Then George Washington, his brother, came by and said "You really need some new tools." "Yes I sure do, would you have any?" John asked. "Yes I do," said George, "I have a garage full."

John took what he needed and he made a perfect time traveler.

John was very excited and a little nervous to start it up, but he did it anyway and the lights went out and darkness settled in.

Suddenly the lights went back on and he was back in prehistoric time.

He was immediately greeted by the Flintstones. They had tea and biscuits and light conversation.

After getting some much needed rest the Flintstones taught John how to train dinosaurs.

Later the next day Wilma and Betty taught him how to make clothes out of dinosaur hides, and Barney taught him how to hunt and kill dinosaurs.

Soon he missed his brother George and said goodbye to the Flintstones.

He went back home to the future and never went back. For the rest of his life he told stories of his adventures.

Nobody ever believed John but George learned a valuable lesson about telling lies and we all know how his story goes.

MY WORLD
STAVROULA ECONOMAKOS, AGE 9

The Color of my planet would be orange.
The laws would be....
    No Smoking
    No littering
    No Homework on Friday
    No Tests
    Nobody can be silent.
    No bad words.
    Read books.
    You have to have fun.

For breakfast we can eat cereal, waffles, pancakes, bacon, sausage, eggs, Irish breakfast and anything else we want.
For lunch, sandwiches, pizza, chicken nuggets and our favorite foods.
For dinner we can have spaghetti, hamburgers, fish and anything else we can think of.

For dessert we can have all the sugary things we
can think of.
But if they can't think of anything else, the ice
cream truck comes around every day.
The weather is mostly sunny, it rains sometimes,
and it rarely snows.
That is what my planet would be like.

ODE TO CHRISTINA
WISSAL HAJAZEHAF, AGE 7

O Christina
You are nice.
You make me
Laugh. You are
A little silly.
You make me
Happy when I am
Sad. You also
Keep company.
You are my friend.

THE BOY, THE SNAKE, AND THE BALL
MAYA HERNANDEZ, AGE 6

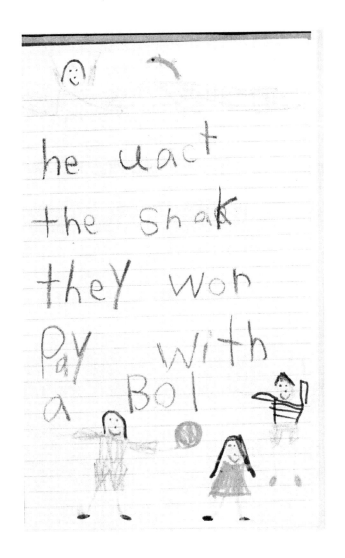

he uact
the snak
they wor
pay with
a Bol

28

BEWARE OF HUMANS
ISABELLA HUANG, AGE 10

Hi! My name is Crocie. I'm a crocodile. Once I was caught and almost died. I was sleeping and suddenly I heard someone crying for help. Crodie, my neighbor, got shot by a hunter. Then, a net fell on me, and I fainted. When I woke up, I heard a hunter say, "That looks like it might cost millions." When I heard that, it freaked me out. Suddenly, I remembered my chewing skills, and chewed my way out. When I got out and stepped on the ground, an alarm started ringing. It sounded something like this, "Crocodile on the move, go catch it!" Then I picked up my right foot and saw a red button on ground. A hunter was heading straight for me with a gun in his hand. Then I ran for my life and stopped to catch my breath, then BAM! I thought I was dead, but when I opened my eyes: I saw that he trapped me in a non-chewable metal cage. That night while I was sleeping, something shook me, and it was Crodie. He opened my cage and got me out. When we reached our home, he told me the whole story. The next day everything was back to normal.

MY LIFE
ISABELLA HUANG, AGE 10

My life was regular until one day I was drawing a cat. When I was finished, it licked me. I looked at my body and I had fur all over me. I was a cat. I scratched my paw and I was myself again. I remember in Harry Potter a person who can change into an animal was called an Animagi. Did it happen? Was I one of them? I traced the part again and...it licked me and I was a cat again. I scratched my paw, and I was myself again. (I didn't want my parents to worry so I didn't tell them.)

With my new power I can do almost anything. In the morning, I can talk to birds and animals. One night in cat form, I crept out and asked my fish what do they think of the food, and they said it was fine, which made me happy. I didn't use my power unless it was really urgent.

THINGS THAT MATTER
ALEXIA KOUGENTAKIS, AGE 7

The museum matters,
The animals matter.
Everything in the world matters.
The Pilgrims matter,
The Native Americans matter.
My dog matters,
My family matters.
My bones matter.
I love things.
My house and my puppy matter.
My friend's baby matters,
My life matters.
My teachers matter.

O TRAILER
ALEXIA KOUGENTAKIS, AGE 7

O trailer why are you so dirty
O trailer is your front door so irritated
O trailer why are you so small
O trailer why cant you fit in with the other trailers
O trailer why are you mad
O trailer why can't you move
O trailer you are so pretty
O trailer why are you so uncolored
O trailer is your girlfriend in the campground
O trailer can you look like a hotel
O trailer why does your light not work
O trailer can you play football
O trailer can you be pretty

SNOW
PASCALE LEONE, AGE 10

Snow smells like hot chocolate.
Snow sounds like angels flying down to Earth.
Snow tastes like a quick gulp of cold water.
Snow feels like freezing sugar.
Snow looks like cold cotton.

SOUNDS
PASCALE LEONE, AGE 10

The waves crashed onto the shore.
I smell the salty air and then...silence.

Sitting in the airport waiting,
Listening to different languages,
Finally, the plane.

Bong, bong, bong
The church bells rang
On Christmas morning.

I sat in the restaurant
Tasting the coffee,
Old music blaring.

I rocked the baby
Trying to comfort her,
No quiet.

"I want a cookie!" he screamed.
Ahhh!
Let me relax.

Chirp, chirp, chirp
Mockingbird squawking,
Keeping me up.

MY WORLD
PASCALE LEONE, AGE 10

In my world, everyone would own a penthouse.
There would be NO hobos. There would be
professional cops and robber teams. The t.v.
channel Cartoon Network is BANNED. In my
world, mean coaches are Banned! Schools teach
many languages. If you don't have pizza at least 3
times a week, you get shipped off to prison.
Younger inmates can get an education (not the best
one, though.) Ice cream parlors must be every 2
blocks. Arirang must be every 5 blocks. Every
child must have 40 books. All pools must have
water slides. Disney is in every town. Penthouses
are pale pink or white. You are immortal.

IMAGINE
TRISTAN LEONE, AGE 8

Imagine we have no gravity.
Imagine no school.
Imagine time machines.
Imagine there were no girls.
Imagine no parents.
Imagine you can fly.
Imagine me and Che.

I SHOULD KNOW
TRISTAN LEONE, AGE 8

I should know how to do my times tables.
Luka should know how to play baseball.
I should know how to kiss.
My mom should know how to get me the PSP go
      and 3DSI's.

FOOD
TRISTAN LEONE, AGE 8

'Twas the night before Thanksgiving and all
      through the house,
Not a creature was stirring,
Not even a turkey.
The children were nestled
All stuck in their beds,
Dreaming of Slappy New Year
Eating their heads.

They fell out of their beds.

DREAM
SILVIA MANCINI, AGE 7

I have a dream that everyone should not be called
names.

The reason why I believe this is because it makes
people feel sad.

People should be called the names that their
parents gave them.

If people say something mean, they should be sent
to the Principal.

I think this is a good idea because it sometimes
happens in my classroom.

I dream that everyone will be kind to each other.

NATURE'S SNOW
SILVIA MANCINI, AGE 7

Snow is water, it cannot come from a tree,

but it can fall from the sky.

I love snow because it is nature and nature is
beautiful.

When I play with snow I'm playing with nature.

EARTH
SILVIA MANCINI, AGE 7

I know how to paint a picture, but I don't know
how to put paint on a palette

I know how to buy clothes, but I don't know how
to find good sizes

I know how to paint nails, but I don't know how to
do "French"

I like to buy nail polish, but I don't know how to
pick a nice color

I know how to play "Just Dance" on the Wii, but I
don't know how to do the "Salsa"

I know how to walk, but I can't walk on the moon

I like gravity, but I don't know how to float on
Earth

SOUNDS
BRIDIN MCCANN, AGE 10

An old car's motor as the car drives,
And slowly comes to a stop.
An airplane or the inside of a seashell.

A very noisy room or place where everyone is
    talking.
A swim meet or an airport.

A loud bell ringing on the hour.
A church bell or a gang from a movie.

Someone playing guitar,
Pascale's dad or music.

Someone crying,
A baby at birth or someone having a tantrum.

People screaming.
A Bounce U party or girls vs. boys.

A bird singing.
A mockingbird or a bird singin a song of joy.

THE DREAM
BRIDIN MCCANN, AGE 10

POEM: I time traveled here and there...
I saw me in the past and in the future.
HHEELLPP!
STORY: Marcia ran and ran through the hot sticky
place. Something was following me!
Ahhh! I woke up feeling so scared. Beep beep
beep my alarm clock went off. "Marcia,"
my mom called.
I got up and started getting ready for school.
It was another weary Monday morning.

WHO I AM
BRIDIN MCCANN, AGE 10

I swim like a dolphin gliding
Through the water.
I imagine myself floating through the air.
I see blue of the water
And the floor of the pool.
I smell chlorine.
I taste nothing.
I hear splashes my own and other people's.
I feel the water pushing against me.

IMAGINATION (AN ACROSTIC POEM)
SADIE MCCANN, AGE 7

Imagine me, Fiona, and Amanda were triplets.
Make the world a better place.
An amazing world around us.
Great things around us.
Imagine we got 10 Christmas presents.
No homework or any work.
And love the Earth.
Take a chance to help the world.
Imagine it was Christmas every day.
Oh, be a best friend.
Never be shy.

THE CRAZY STORY
SADIE MCCANN, AGE 7

I play like my shoes thunder.
I my shoes like a thunder play.
I thunder like a play my shoes.

I beat like a music disappears.
I music like a disappearing beat.
I disappear like a beat music.

I help like a battle thunders.
I battle like a thunder helps.
I thunder like a help battles.

I swim like a puzzle writes.
I a puzzle like a write swims.
I write like a swims a puzzle.

I talk like a homework smiles.
I homework like a smiles talk.
I smile like a talk homework.

I smile like a magic poem.
I magic like a poem smiles.
I poem like a smiles magic.

I poem like a puzzle battles.
I puzzle like a battle's poem.
I battle like a poem a puzzle.

MY WORLD
SADIE MCCANN, AGE 7

My world would be called Friends' World.
Everybody would be Puffles and your favorite
color would be the color of your Puffle. And in
every store that you went to, there would be ice
cream. And you can have multi-colored for your
Puffle. My friend Max is multi-colored, black and
white. My other friend Frances is purple, and I am
green. And the only car you could get would be a
limo and a punch buggy. And if you had a big
family, there could be an attached punch buggy.
And people would never die. And it would always
be a nice day out. And Santa would come once a
month. You would have your birthday once a
month. And at most houses they would have a
pool. So almost everywhere you go you needed to
bring a bathing suit. And you would only have
school on Mondays and Tuesdays. And Fiona's
world would be right next to mine because it is
almost the exact same thing. Elizabeth would own
the world. You would have a play date every day
except on school days. Me, Max, and Frances.
Girls have their middle name not their first name.
Boys would make up their name. Everyone would
be rich. There's more girls than boys in my world.
Boys would have long hats, girls would have short
hats. There is Disneyland in my world. No traffic,
nice food. And there's no winter or snow or rain,
just sunny. You could eat anything in the stores.

But they're not free things. And there's jail if you don't follow the rules. There's not many boys in the world. Once a month you would get a week off from school. And there's no homework if the teachers give homework they would get fired and go to jail. If you're in jail you can't get out unless someone says that they did the crime. I, Elizabeth, own most things in the world. Girls have to wear a diamond necklace. Everything in my world would be expensive. It would be hard to get things because it would be expensive. All of these things are laws in my world.

WHAT I DO
LEILA MULLARKEY, AGE 5

People think I have big cheeks.
And I do.
I love the snow.
When I go outside in the snow,
It is cold out.

IMAGINE
LEILA MULLARKEY, AGE 5

Imagine
If I had a horse,
If people didn't have arms,
If people are invisible.
I hope for a sister.
I hope work and school are not real.

Peace.

MY CHARACTER
FIONA PFAFFLIN, AGE 7

Her name is Agene. She is 26 years old. She is a
girl, but she looks like a bear. She goes to college.
She lives in an apartment building. She has two
kids and her boyfriend is the weirdest guy ever.
Her best friend in the whole world is Sarah. Her
fear is to drive. Her wish is to be famous. My
character likes to sing and dance. She is very shy
and expects things a lot. Her favorite color is
black. She wears fur every day. Her skin color is
brown. I hate her because her hair is a weird style
and her shirt is weird looking and she looks like
Britney Spears. She likes to eat hot dogs and fish.
For drinks she likes Sprite and water. I do have a
brother. What's my lie?

FIONA'S WORLD
FIONA PFAFFLIN, AGE 7

My world would be named The Fiona's World.
In my world you would always wear purple and
    my friends wouldn't have to pay for
    anything.
You couldn't get into fights including brothers and
    sisters.
And you are in my world without knowing.
Now let's get back to my world.
There is no tv or video games, so you have to read.
You don't die if you rob someone's house you just
    vanish and you will come back next year.
The only car you can get is a minivan or a
    limousine.
You can only have two children.
In my world you will vanish if you have three
    children.
Nobody can see the president or if you're famous
    your mom can't see you.
Santa will come every week and on your birthday.
You have to wear a ponytail everyday except for
    picture day.
You only have school on Thursday.
Sadie would have a million dollars and more.
You would have a playdate every day except for
    school day.
Sunday doesn't exist, it means it is sunny in my
    world.
And my best friend Sadie is famous.
Saturday is the only day you have ice cream and
    cupcakes.

Pascale has two hundred dollars.
And your dreams are always good on Mondays
   not Saturdays.
Girls have to wear a necklace and boys bandana,
   unless they want to wear a necklace.
You have to wear a top hat inside and outside.
Everyday you would eat salmon, steak, chicken,
   burgers, pizza.
You have to draw at least for an hour.
The moon is orange and your skin is orange.
You have to have blonde hair.
You have to have blue eyes and black rubber
   bands.
There is no such thing as jail in my world.
Your school is the color pink.
You have to have a pet dog or cat.
And wear sneakers or ballet slippers every day.
Your clothes are from The Childrens Place.
There are playgrounds everywhere you go.
You have to go to Disney World every week for at
   least a day.
There are more girls than boys.
You have to wear beautiful shirts except for boys
   they wear plain shirts.
Everybody has to have an Expo board.
Girls have to have earrings.
You have to have the diamond earrings.
You have to have lipstick for girls not boys.
You have to like water.
All the movies are about me, Fiona.
Boys look weird and girls look beautiful.

All animals are colorful.
You eat for breakfast waffles with syrup or nutella.
Norah has 20,000 dollars and she's famous.
Everybody has freckles.
You have to wear a watch.
You have to be healthy.
You have to go to the movies on movie day which
      is Tuesday.
Vesuvio is the only pizza place and Five Guys is
      the only burger store.
Hana is the salmon place.
That's my world!

LOVE IS...
HANNAH PUELLE, AGE 8

Love is red, purple, pink
Love is flowers
Love is hearts
Love is donuts and hot chocolate
Love is happy
Love is play dates
Love is going on dates
Love is a swim meet with ice cream at the end
Love is moms and dads
Love is peace
Love is Christina
Love is family
Love is Valentine's Day

THINGS THAT ARE DULL
AMANDA SAHADI, AGE 8

A dull night is exciting,
A dull morning is lazy.
A dull evening is happy.
A dull midnight is tiring.

WHO I AM
AMANDA SAHADI, AGE 8

People think I am interested in science. I like to
do experiments. I wear green goggles. I use
different colors. My experiments are not all
useful. I like to pour things. I use food coloring.
The food coloring is all different colors. When
you pour it in it looks different from when you
already poured it. The food coloring looks shiny.
The different colors are orange, white, green, blue,
yellow and many more.

RHYMING PANDAS

AMANDA SAHADI, AGE 8

My name is Amanda,
I never saw a panda
I think pandas have pretty noses,
They should never use hoses
Don't let them get wet,
Because I will never see a sunset
Pandas sleep in beds,
Their noses never get red
Pandas eat bamboo,
When they sneeze they go achoo!!!!!!!!!!!!
They would never be so loud,
Unless I saw a cloud
I always have a dream of them inside a stream,
I always see some flowers
I think that they have power,
To give some to pandas
A Christmas present from Santa
They can be snuggly,
As close as it is to cuddly
They have furry hair,
When I had a nightmare
I would hate to see them with a kangaroo,
Especially you know, in a zoo
I wish I could see a panda right now!

10 THINGS I SHOULD KNOW HOW TO DO BUT I DON'T
VICTORIA SAHADI, AGE 9

1. whistling
2. snapping fingers
3. charging my ipod
4. how to play Mouse Trap
5. read books over 700 pages
6. sing
7. dance
8. get 100% on a math test
9. do flip turns in the water
10. do cartwheels

MY DREAM ROOM
VICTORIA SAHADI, AGE 9

My dream room would be a Halloween Room. It
would be dark and cold. There would be shadows
on the wall that don't belong to anyone and ghosts
floating around. There would be a huge selection
of costumes and at least five different types of one
costume. You wouldn't be able to enter unless
you got a costume. When you got one, you can
open a chest the size of a big table that is filled to
the top with a million or more pieces of candy. It
would magically refill, so if you ate the whole
thing in one visit, the next time you go back, it
would be full. The Halloween Room would have
jack-o-lanterns and signs that say things like
"Beware of Bats." This is what the Halloween
Room would be like.

SUMMER (A LIMERICK, CINQUAIN, AND POEM)
VICTORIA SAHADI, AGE 9

It was a hot summer day
The children came to play
Playing ball in the beach
When it fell out of reach.
The ball was melted by the sun's hot ray.

Summer
Hot, fun
Eating, swimming, playing
Play at the beach
August.

Summer's here!
It's time to play
Time to be
Outside all day.
Time for games,
And time for fun!
Time to be out in the sun!
School is out!
Now you can shout!
Now it's just a memory-the pencils and books
The reading and writing and mean teachers' looks.
The games and the parties
And visiting Spain,
The yelling,
The shouting,
It's never gonna rain.
We're free and we're glad

That Summer is here!
Let's have fun!
After all, it just
Comes once a year!

.

WHAT I AM MADE OF
LUKA SILVA, AGE 8

I am made of kicking balls in the goal.
I am made of swimming fast to be a champion.
I am made of kicking someone's ball.
I am made of eating pizza and ice cream.
I am made of hearing rock and roll.
I am made of going to the park every day.
I am made of going to school every day too.
I am made of being a good friend to my friend
       Tristan.
I am made of Brazil.

WHAT I NOTICED
LUKA SILVA, AGE 8

I noticed *Diary of a Wimpy Kid* on a table.

I noticed that kids were playing games on the
       computer.

I noticed there were kids DVD's on a giant shelf.

I noticed a little girl that was 6 playing on the iPad

I noticed there was a poster with the book called
       The Red Pyramid.

I noticed that Tristan was lorded by a DS.

I noticed that Sunny D was hanging out with
Coca-cola.

FEELINGS
LUCIA SNAJDR, AGE 5

A dull night is bad.
It is bad because you have toys and you pretend to
be bored.

An exciting night is having a party for dinner.

An exciting morning is having waffles for
breakfast.
An exciting morning is not going to school.
An exciting morning is not changing into your real
clothes.

A dull morning is you have to have cereal.
A dull morning is a rain storm.

A dull afternoon is not having your friends over.
A dull afternoon is going to school.
A dull afternoon is having no sushi.
A dull afternoon is having your tree get cut down.
A dull afternoon is having your mommy go to
work.

An exciting afternoon is having a baby.
An exciting afternoon is having new furniture.
An exciting afternoon is having a pet.
An exciting afternoon is doing your play time.

WHAT I WOULD CHANGE ABOUT THE WORLD
LUCIA SNAJDR, AGE 5

I would make it so everyone would know
     everyone.

I imagine the world being strong and safe.

I imagine I would live in a hotel.

I imagine people could ride on top of clouds.

I imagine there was every night beautiful
     fireworks.

I imagine that there would be no trees cut down.

THE BEACH
FATMA SOLIMAN, AGE 9

The place that I like is where the waves come up, and when they make shadows. Where you play in the sand and might get a pail or shovel. The place has the sun, the burning hot sun, but don't worry, there's water to cool you down. It is a place with green squiggly colorful sheets.

It's where the seagulls are. They search for food on hot burning sand. It's where sea and land meet. You will see life all around you. It's a place you have fun.

THINGS I SAW
CHRISTINA STERN, AGE 7

1. books
2. bathroom
3. kids
4. kids' book
5. old people
6. people talking
7. chairs
8. Christina's boots
9. Lucy's shoe
10. emergency exit
11. elevator
12. emergency bells
13. buttons
14. custodian closet
15. bags
16. windows
17. cars

MY KITCHEN
CHRISTINA STERN, AGE 7

This kitchen is the color white, the little doors is
brown, the walls white.

IMAGINE
GIULIANA TEPEDINO, AGE 7

Imagine your classroom was a jungle.
Imagine your house was a zoo.
Imagine your class got 10,000 yellow tickets in
     one day.
Imagine you kept on turning into a bat and never
     stopped.
What if a pig sneaked into your house?
Imagine someone went to school naked.
Imagine you had one thousand pages of
     homework.
Imagine there was such a big snowstorm, school
     was closed for a week.

BEING
GIULIANA TEPEDINO, AGE 7

Being happy is pink.
Being sad is blue.
Being mad is grey.
Being excited is red.
Being afraid is black.
Being happy smells like a chocolate heart.
Being sad smells like a sour lemon.
Being mad smells like a strawberry smoothie.
Being excited smells like chocolate chip cookies
        baking in the oven.
Being afraid smells like a stinky forest.

YELLOW IS
JEANIE TRAMONTANO, AGE 6

Yellow is joy.
Yellow is fun.
Yellow is cool.
Yellow is the sun.

Yellow is pretty.
Yellow is a flower.
Yellow is gorgeous.
Yellow smells like flowers.

It talks to me and says:
"I am glad that I am your favorite color.
Tell other people to like yellow too.
I am glad that you are my friend."

Yellow sounds like hip-hop music.
Yellow tastes like Oreos.
I feel like yellow is a real person to me.

WHAT I SEE!
KATHY YAN, AGE 9

What I see, an awesome library filled of books
with different genres written from all different
authors. Also Rochelle wanting me to make an
angry face.

What I see is the clock and it is 3:30 so we have to
go to violin!

What I see is Isabella and Rochelle fighting.

65